MONSTERS!

MONSTERS!

Draw Your Own
Mutants, Freaks & Creeps

Jay Stephens

LARK BOOKS

A Division of Sterling Publishing Co., Inc.
New York

Editor
VERONIKA ALICE GUNTER

Creative Director
CELIA NARANJO

Design & Production
THOM GAINES

Cover Design
JAY STEPHENS

Library of Congress Cataloging-in-Publication Data

Stephens, Jay, 1971-
  Monsters! : draw your own mutants, freaks & creeps /
    by Jay Stephens. --
1st ed.
    p. cm.
Includes index.
ISBN 1-57990-935-3 (hardcover)
1. Monsters in art. 2. Drawing--Technique. 1. Title.
NC825.M6S74 2007
743'.8--dc22

2006036104

10 9 8 7 6 5 4 3 2 1

First Edition

Published by Lark Books
A Division of Sterling Publishing Co., Inc.
387 Park Avenue South, New York, N.Y. 10016

© 2007, Jay Stephens

Distributed in Canada by Sterling Publishing,
c/o Canadian Manda Group, 165 Dufferin Street
Toronto, Ontario, Canada M6K 3H6

Distributed in the United Kingdom by GMC Distribution Services,
Castle Place, 166 High Street, Lewes, East Sussex, England BN7 1XU

Distributed in Australia by Capricorn Link (Australia) Pty Ltd.,
P.O. Box 704, Windsor, NSW 2756 Australia

If you have questions or comments about this book, please contact:
Lark Books, 67 Broadway, Asheville, NC 28801
(828) 253-0467

Manufactured in China
All rights reserved

ISBN 13: 978-1-57990-935-2 (hardcover)
ISBN 10: 1-57990-935-3 (hardcover)
ISBN 13: 978-1-60059-178-5 (paperback)
ISBN 10: 1-60059-178-7 (paperback)

For information about custom editions, special sales, and premium and corporate
purchases, please contact Sterling Special Sales Department at 800-805-5489 or
specialsales@sterlingpub.com.

CONTENTS

Welcome to a Weird World of Monsters

Good evening, fellow fiends! If you've ever dreamt up your own mutants, freaks, and creeps, you're not alone. I've always loved to draw uncanny characters and to tell spooky stories—especially ones that really creep me out! Everyone enjoys a little fright now and then. Besides, creepy crawly creatures are cool!

In this book you'll find all you need to begin creating and drawing your very own spine-tingling weirdos (or friendly freaks). Along the way, you'll meet dozens of my monsters. With step-by-step instructions for drawing a bunch of them, this book will help you practice the skills you need to bring your own monsters to life. And every page gives you ideas for creating a brand new freak! Grab a few supplies before you get started:

- Some plain, white paper (8½ x 11-inch computer paper works well)
- A regular 2H, 2HB, or 2B pencil
- A pen or fine-tipped marker (black, if possible, but dark blue will do)
- A good eraser (gum or plastic are best)
- Colored markers, pencils, or water-based paints
- OR a scanner and a computer with illustration software

Drawing is Easy

You'll use the pencil to lightly draw all sorts of marks and lines on your paper—zigzags, circles, straight lines, curved ones. (I call these construction lines.) The pen or marker is what you'll use to trace your best monster drawings. (I call this inking the final drawing.) Then you use the eraser to get rid of the lines you aren't using. (That's why none of your marks have to be perfect.) There are lots of ways to add color to your final drawings. I put a whole section about color at the end of the book.

Part of learning to draw is mastering the marks you make on paper. The more you draw, the more confident you'll become. So use this book and draw a lot! But your hands will only get you so far. You've got to use your head. Imagination is the most important part of making a picture. Don't just let your thoughts run wild—chase them down a dark alley...or to wherever your monsters hang!

—Jay Stephens

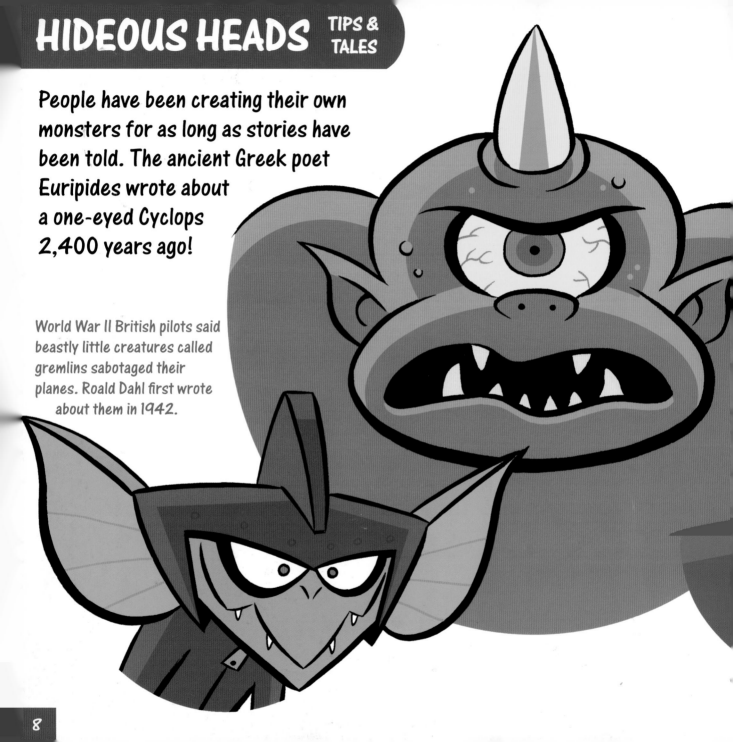

People have been creating their own monsters for as long as stories have been told. The ancient Greek poet Euripides wrote about a one-eyed Cyclops 2,400 years ago!

World War II British pilots said beastly little creatures called gremlins sabotaged their planes. Roald Dahl first wrote about them in 1942.

Mary Shelley was a teenager when she had the nightmare that inspired her to create the famous Frankenstein monster. Her novel was published nearly 200 years ago.

The ancient Egyptians often drew animal heads on human bodies, like the jackal-headed god of the underworld—Anubis. The wrong kind of head on a body can look pretty strange.

The Headless Horseman didn't even have a head! He had to make due with a jack-o'-lantern.

I'm just a walking head!

Heads up! I like to start my creatures from the top down. Human heads tend to be round. An unusual shape looks monstrous!

If you get stuck for ideas, try scribbling! A doodle can easily be turned into a freak—with a little imagination.

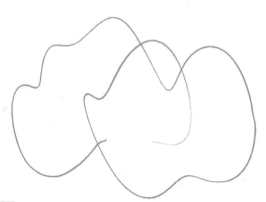

The Slink Brothers insist that three heads are better than one! Simon Slink is bold and giggly. Sidney Slink likes to hide behind his creepy hairdo.

Even a beautiful head can look bizarre, depending on what it's attached to. This long-necked yokai called Rokurokubi is a perfect example.

Finding a head where it isn't supposed to be is weird. Seymour Slink is in a sleeve!

These Japanese goblin spirits are called yokai.

The eyes are the most expressive part of the face—and the most important to think about when creating your monster.

All of Peepster's 10 eyes are exactly the same shape and size. But with just a few lines, you can completely change the expressions.

Grumpy, angry eyes are made with straight lines pointing down in the middle.

Big eyeballs and pupils make a face look cute. Eyelashes help, too.

Thin, slanting eyes make a face sinister.

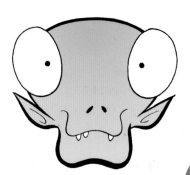

Eyes set really close together make a creature look silly and unintelligent.

Eyes set very far apart look inhuman—more like a bug, fish, or reptile.

Double frowny curves right through the middle create sleepy, squinty eyes.

Want sad, worried eyes? Draw a curve through each eyeball, curving slightly upward, toward the middle.

Here are more eye-deas...

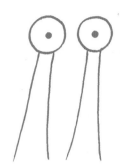

Apes have thick brows and beady eyes.

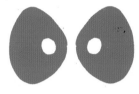

Dark eyes with white pupils look creepy!

Small pupils and curves around the outside give you scared, surprised eyeballs.

Snails have eye stalks.

Octopus eyes are bulbous with weirdly shaped pupils.

Curved, leaf-shaped eyes look spooky!

You can create eyes without eyeballs. Here's what it looks like to draw pupils only.

Snake eyes are round with long, thick pupils.

Wobbly pupils and mismatched eyes make for a dizzy, loony look.

Look around you for inspiration. Car taillights make great monster eyes!

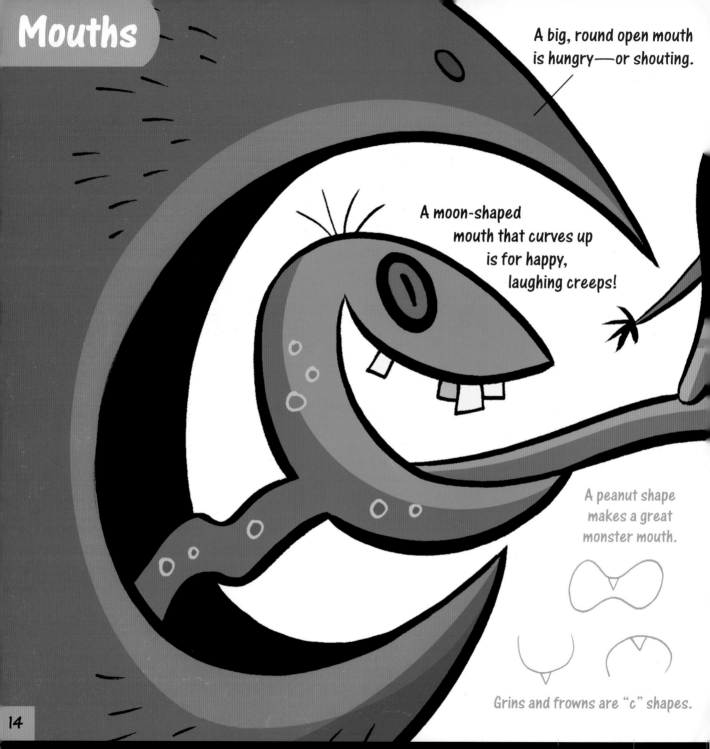

Mouths

A big, round open mouth is hungry—or shouting.

A moon-shaped mouth that curves up is for happy, laughing creeps!

A peanut shape makes a great monster mouth.

Grins and frowns are "c" shapes.

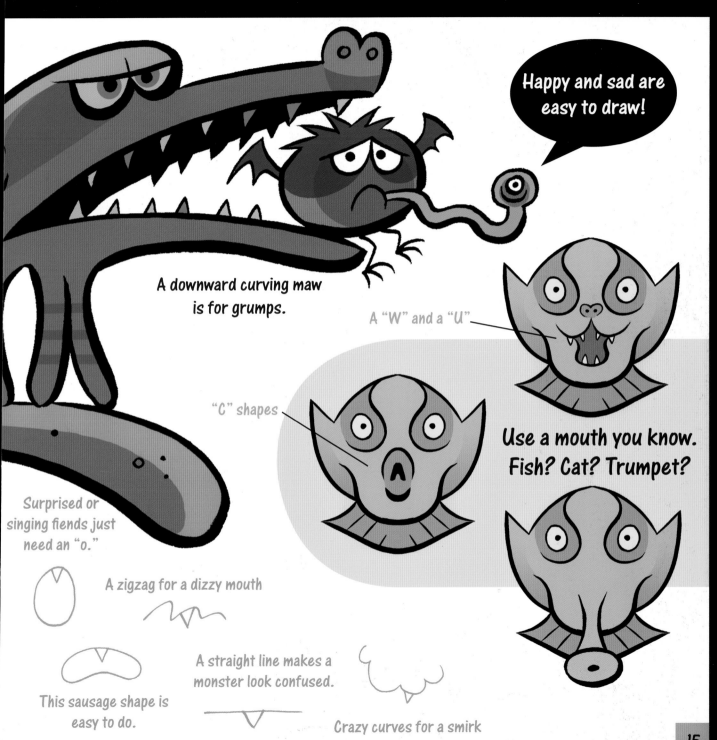

Happy and sad are easy to draw!

A downward curving maw is for grumps.

A "W" and a "U"

"C" shapes

Use a mouth you know. Fish? Cat? Trumpet?

Surprised or singing fiends just need an "o."

A zigzag for a dizzy mouth

This sausage shape is easy to do.

A straight line makes a monster look confused.

Crazy curves for a smirk

Noses

Shnozz knows all about noses. He's pretty sure he wouldn't be much of a monster without his 10-foot honker.

Sniff around the house for nose ideas. A pair of scissors works really well!

Ears

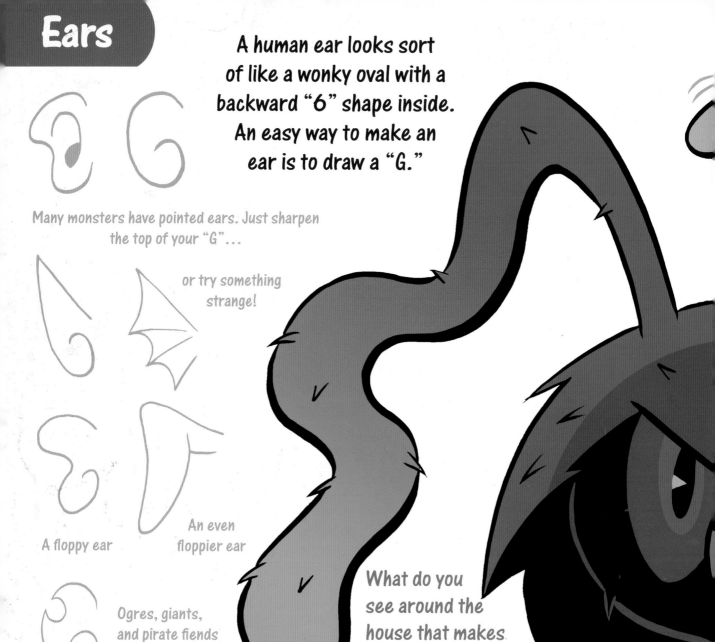

A human ear looks sort of like a wonky oval with a backward "6" shape inside. An easy way to make an ear is to draw a "G."

Many monsters have pointed ears. Just sharpen the top of your "G"...

or try something strange!

A floppy ear

An even floppier ear

Ogres, giants, and pirate fiends often have a piece of their ears missing! An earring is a nice touch.

What do you see around the house that makes a good ear shape? Cup handles? Doorknobs?

Now that you've reached the end of this chapter, you probably have some ideas about creating monster heads.

Imagine what kind of creature you want to make. Does it live in the dark? Under water? Does it breathe fire? Is it fierce or shy? Let these questions help you decide what facial features to choose.

Here are a couple of weirdos to get you started...

This bloodsucker has his eyes on you.

SKEETERMAN

You'd need a really big can of insect repellent to get rid of this campground creep! They say Skeeterman lurks deep in the woods...the sort of middle-of-nowhere spot where scout troops like to set up camp. If you're out there on a muggy summer night, zip up that tent tight. And wear a turtleneck. This werebug bites!

1. Skeeterman's head starts as an oval and a triangle.

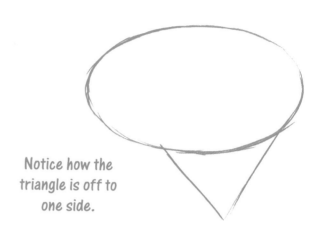

Notice how the triangle is off to one side.

4. Draw a "U" and a "V" for a big one-tooth grin.

Create his hair and collar with zigzag lines.

Draw stripes on his nose.

2. To start the nose, make a long "S" shape.

3. Make circles within circles for eyes. Add more nose. Antennae curl up from the top of the head.

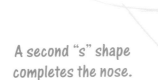

A second "s" shape completes the nose.

5. Now create your final drawing by tracing your best construction lines with a pen or marker.

Erase the lighter lines if you want.

6. Now color him.

Draw this walking freakshow.

LITTLE STRANGER

Sometimes you'll see this weirdo out the window of the subway—usually while you're in a tunnel. Little Stranger also likes peeking into airplane windows, and peering out of locked grandfather clocks. If he asks you to let him in (or out), please just say, "NO!"

1. Draw a square on top of an oval.

An oval is almost a circle.

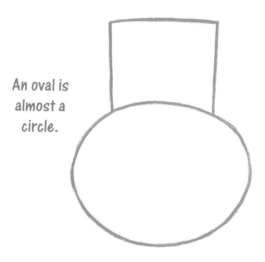

4. The hair is just an upside-down "V" in the middle, plus straight lines on the sides.

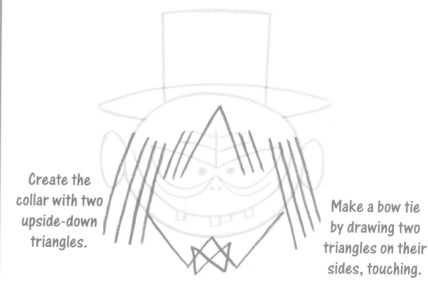

Create the collar with two upside-down triangles.

Make a bow tie by drawing two triangles on their sides, touching.

2. Add a skinny oval for the hat brim. Create eyes and ears.

Slanted eyes and beady pupils

Add big ears: draw a "C" shape on each side of the head.

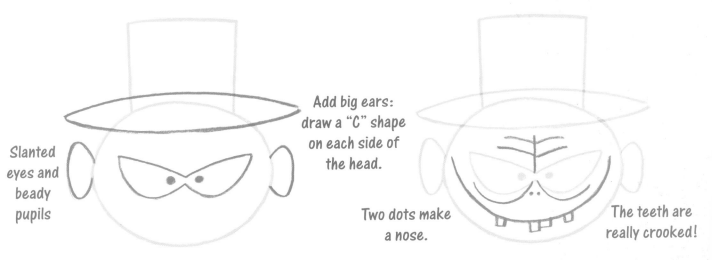

3. Wrinkles are just a few uneven lines, plus a vertical line up from between the eyes.

Two dots make a nose.

The teeth are really crooked!

5. Ready to use ink? Trace the construction lines you want to keep.

Erase the lines you don't need.

6. Time for some icky color to complete this creep!

If you thought monster heads were weird, wait until you see their bodies!

Stories of supernatural creeps come from all over the world. In Romania, some people believe witches die and become vampires called Strigoi Mort.

Ancient Gnostic writings describe a freaky creature called Abraxas. It had the head of a rooster, body of a man, and legs made of snakes.

The Abominable Snowman is an ape-man that might actually exist. The first Westerner to spot what the locals called Yeti was British explorer B. H. Hodson who saw it during an 1832 expedition in the Himalayas.

Look around your neighborhood for bizarre body ideas. A weird old house, an automobile, or a dead tree might inspire an idea for a monster.

Some freaky creatures don't have bodies...like ghosts!

25

Bodies

The Knockniks hang out inside your gutters. They make all those clunking sounds you hear at night. They come in all shapes and sizes...

A big, roundish body with a face near the top looks chunky and tough.

A thinner body looks sneaky.

Scribbles are great inspirations for crazy body ideas.

A big head with a face near the bottom looks brainy and mutated.

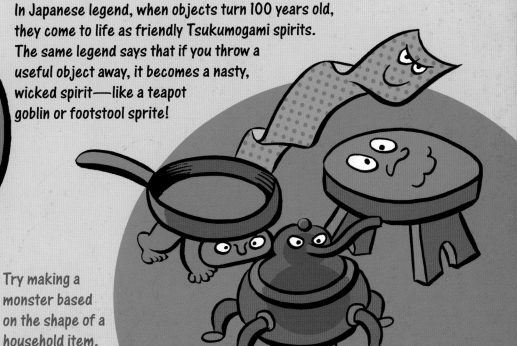

In Japanese legend, when objects turn 100 years old, they come to life as friendly Tsukumogami spirits. The same legend says that if you throw a useful object away, it becomes a nasty, wicked spirit—like a teapot goblin or footstool sprite!

Try making a monster based on the shape of a household item.

27

Arms

If your backpack suddenly feels much heavier than usual, a sinister Backpacula might have moved in. No one knows if there's more than an arm to this creature, because that's all anyone has ever seen.

The kind of arms you give your monster says a lot about what it can do.

Thin or wobbly arms look weak.

Most arms end in hands—or claws. Will your freaky creature have fingers? Tentacles? Razor-sharp blades?

Make a regular hand with a square and five rectangles. A circle and five loops work, too.

Curvy shapes can make a sharp hand or a claw.

Try elongated fingers or webbed hands.

Long or thick arms look strong.

Weird, wrong arms like these look monstrous.

Legs

Human legs make up about half of the body. Your monster's legs can do anything you want!

Let's try out some leg shapes...

Solid

Buggy

Short

Feline

Lots

Elephant

Scary Larry sneaks around at night eating road signs, so nobody knows when to stop the next morning. He covers a lot of ground on his long, creepy legs. Fences don't stop Larry, no sir!

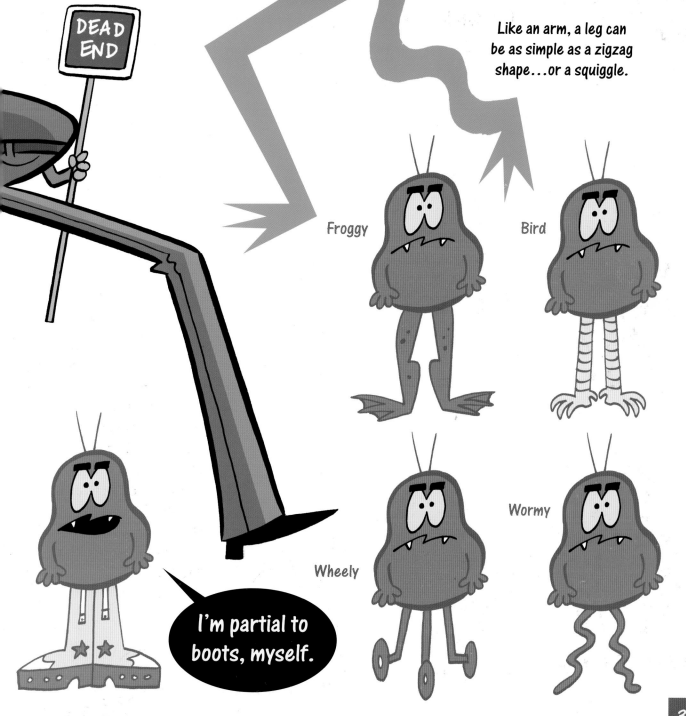

Quadrupeds

Draw an unexpected head on a friendly four-legged animal (a quadruped) to transform it into a monster.

Create your own original four-legged freaks. I took the body of a horse and added a face so ugly it could break a mirror. I call it Goblicorn.

The ancient Egyptian Sphinx had the head of a man and the body of a lion. He also talked in riddles. How will your monster talk?

Look at the animals at the zoo or in picture books for ideas for your quadruped monsters.

This haunting hill beast has the body of a llama and the head of a skeleton. It's called—what else?— Skullama!

With a few adjustments, I bet your pet would make a good weirdo!

Extra Limbs

How many limbs are too many? On a freaky creature, you can never have too many arms or legs!

Bad Luck Butch has 13 arms and legs…the better to pinch, punch, slap, kick, and grab you with!

Fewer limbs can be just as scary as more.

I'm really good at sports!

Insects have six legs. A creepy-crawly pest like a roach is a great inspiration for a monster!

Arachnids (like spiders, scorpions, and ticks) and octopuses all have eight legs. What other creatures have additional appendages?

Tails

A tail can add lots of character to your monstrous creation. Let's try a few...

Devil or dragon

Rat or lizard

Lion or donkey

Tiger

Scorpion stinger

Yikes!

This Coilnick uses its tail to move around.

How can you tell the difference between a regular fox and a Japanese fox spirit called Kitsune? Kitsune has extra tails!

Wings

Horace has to flap his big wings pretty hard to get in and out of his belfry—he's carved out of solid stone!

Some more ideas that might fly...

Bat wings are the most popular for monsters.

Fly wings—ick!

Butterfly wings are almost too pretty, but they look freaky on a head.

Bird wings

Do you have lots of new ideas for how your monster will look and move—and what it can do?

So what kind of body, arms, legs, tail, or wings will you create for this creeptacular freak?

Here are a couple of bizarre monster bodies to practice...

What if her hair were wings?

CREATE IT!

Put together what you know to draw this ghoulish gorilla.

SPOOK OOK

Did you hear that? That thumping in the attic? The people who lived here before you were circus performers. They had a pet gorilla. The gorilla's ghost is haunting the attic...banging around and waiting for someone to come up and play with him. Don't believe me? Go see for yourself!

1. Spook Ook starts as a head and body. Draw a large, upside-down egg shape. Now draw an oval off to one side.

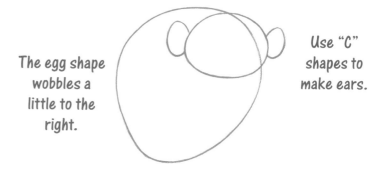

The egg shape wobbles a little to the right.

Use "C" shapes to make ears.

4. Spook Ook's face is made from curves. His body is ghostly—it disappears like a puff of smoke.

The ghostly tail is made of one squiggly line on top and one straight line below.

The nose is three "U's" connected at the top.

2. Create his arms with gentle curves and straight lines. Two blocky shapes rough out his fists.

Make the fists big!

3. This body's covered with hair, so show the shaggy parts with zigzag lines.

Finish the fists with three fingers and a thumb each.

5. Use a dark color to trace the lines you want to keep.

To get a glowing ghost effect, only trace the face with black. Do the rest with a bold blue or green. Then erase your construction lines.

6. Color away!

Use a pale color for the body.

Try drawing the extra limbs and monstrous body of this creep!

DOCKTOPUS

This aquatic beastie likes to nest in the cool, dank shade underneath the dock of your cabin at summer camp. Docktopus hates it when you dangle your feet into the water. So watch out! You're liable to get a very nasty pinch.

1. Start with an oval and a curved bit underneath, sort of like the parts you used for Skeeterman. This is the head and body.

Leave lots of room for all those arms!

4. Docktopus' face is drawn with three "W's," a "W" frown line on the forehead, slanted-in eyes, grump lines on the cheeks, and a squiggle mouth.

A few bubbles help set the scene.

Oops—don't forget the gills on this underwater freak!

2. The arms are five sets of double "S" curves. The legs are four pairs of "V" lines.

Nine limbs?! That makes Docktopus extra freaky.

3. Now for some claws and a face, all made with "C" shapes.

This scalloped line is really six "C's."

The feet are easy: three toes at the end of each bent leg.

5. Use a dark-colored pen or marker to trace your best construction lines.

6. Some cool blue color finishes the job!

You can erase your work lines or just color over them.

Most creepy monsters aren't too neat and clean. They're covered in goo, grime, rivets, and rags! The ancient Minotaur from Greek mythology is a pretty shaggy example.

Mummies and zombies have scraggly hairdos.

Bandages are created with crooked lines.

Zigzags and short lines make a hairy hide.

The mummy of Queen Tiye is all burial dressings and tattered shroud. That's the fashion in royal tombs!

The Bogman has lots of fishy bits sticking out, and some ugly blotches, too.

Draw seaweed with a squiggly line and little ovals for leaves.

The rough stone look of this Creepi Tiki was created by laying the drawing on top of a bumpy old wall and rubbing lightly with a crayon. Wherever you rub, the texture will appear. It works with wood, too!

Here are some simple ways to draw hair...

Moldylocks has a rather fiendish amount of long, shaggy hair. If you like the look of werewolves and tarantulas, you might want your horrible creation to have some fuzz, too!

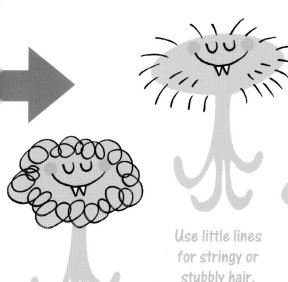

Scribbly coils make for a thick mane.

Use little lines for stringy or stubbly hair.

A few wavy lines and Loxxy has a new pompadour!

Here we have a zigzag shag.

Don't forget—a freaky creep might have hair somewhere odd... like on its hands!

Moustaches can be creepy, too.

A drop of paint can get you started on a fuzzy monster quickly.

Some fantastic creatures, like Rongo here, have thick body armor that protects them from angry mobs of monster-haters!

Try sketching your beastie with a turtle shell or rhino skin. How does it look? You can always start over if you don't like your sketch.

Fish and reptiles have overlapping scales that work as armor.
Here are some easy ways to draw scales.

Try a series of "U" shapes. Be sure to overlap them so that the upper edge of the one underneath touches the lower edge of the one on top.

Create scales with simple zigzag shapes for a jagged, Gila monster* look.

The easiest way to draw scales is with lots of little circles. You can cover your whole monster in them, or just scatter a few around to give a hint of icky texture.

* A Gila monster is a lizard with a huge head and a horrible bite. Its teeth dig in to deliver deadly venom!

Horns & Fins

Nibbs would like to introduce you to some ideas about decorating your monster's body.

Long horns coming from a creature's face are called tusks.

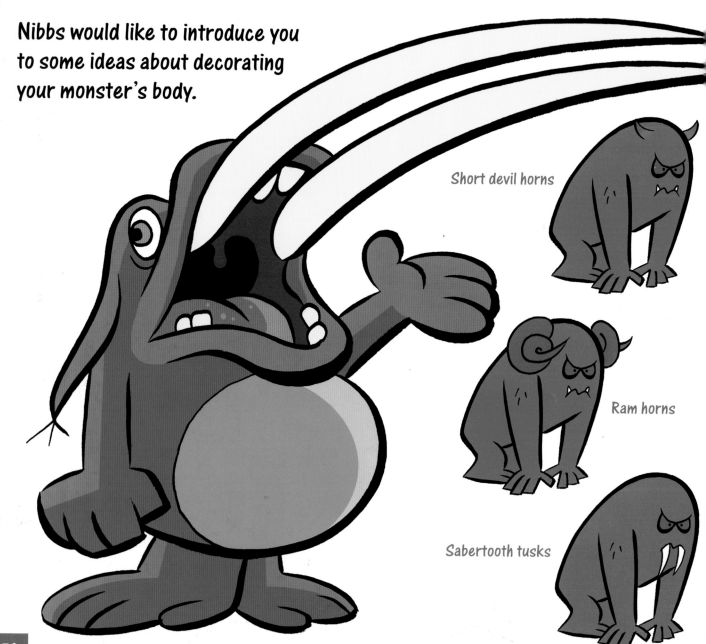

Short devil horns

Ram horns

Sabertooth tusks

A unicorn spike

Adding fins to a creature makes it look aquatic...even if it has arms and legs.

The moose look

An amphibious design, complete with fins and gills

What objects around the house might give you good ideas for more spiky freaks?

Elemental Effects

The four basic elements of nature are Earth, Air, Fire, and Water. But there's nothing natural about the Mutant Quadruplets!

Wick is on fire! Create his hot glow with long, connected "J" curves.

Slop is all wet. That's why I drew his drippiness with wiggly lines.

Chunk is a blockhead. Zigzag cracks and a few dots for pockmarks make a stone-like look.

I think I got too much sun today.

A freaky beast could spit out all sorts of strange stuff—like fire, stinky gases, electricity, or sticky webbing! What else can you think of?

Puffy shapes create Huff's cloudy head. He's a real airhead. Try drawing these effects yourself!

Try your hand at these freaks...

Hairy can be scary.

LURKSTER

Eww! The dark, damp space behind the furnace in the basement has been collecting dust balls, soot, pet hair, and cobwebs for a long, long time. Just look at that disgusting heap! That pile of cruddiness! That—wait—did it just...move?!

1. Lurkster starts off innocently enough with a long, curved shape.

Don't press too hard or it'll be tough to erase these lines later.

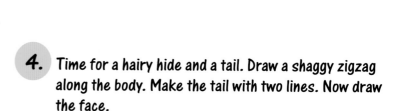

4. Time for a hairy hide and a tail. Draw a shaggy zigzag along the body. Make the tail with two lines. Now draw the face.

Add five little curves on each horn for a nice detail.

One long line creates the brow. Draw a small "C" laying on its side for the eyeball. Draw a larger one for the eye patch. Can you figure out how to draw the pupil and add a couple wrinkles?

2. Create the horns by drawing curved lines connecting at the top with a point.

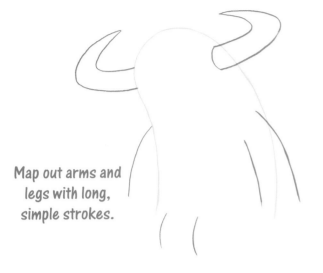

Map out arms and legs with long, simple strokes.

3. The claws are all curved lines. The feet are flat on the bottom and curved on top.

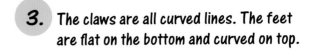

You can begin erasing the construction lines you no longer need.

5. Time to ink! Use a dark ink pen or marker to trace your best construction lines.

I filled in the eye patch, too.

6. Now for the coloring.

AAAAH!

CREATE IT!

Here's a perfectly sloppy, semi-solid scamp.

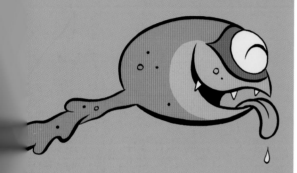

SHLOPPO

Ever wonder what you'd get if you left half a jam sandwich under your bed for three months—next to some rancid gym socks and a leaky size D battery?

Its name is Shloppo. It watches you sleep. When you toss and turn, it rearranges your covers so you are comfy. Feel something warm, wet, and goopy on your skin? It's probably just Shloppo.

1. Draw a flattened circle for the head, and two slightly curved lines for a slender neck.

Be sure to leave lots of room down here for the slimy body.

4. Add details to the eyes and texture to the body.

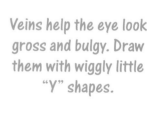

Veins help the eye look gross and bulgy. Draw them with wiggly little "Y" shapes.

Dots and circles all over the body make Shloppo look bubbly.

Add some "U" shaped drips wherever you like.

2. Make one big eyeball circle in the top center of the head. Create a friendly, grinning mouth.

The grin is two stretched "S" curves that meet in the middle.

Draw the blob body any way you like...since Shloppo can change its shape.

3. Draw one arch above the eyeball and one below. Make sure they meet on either side. The teeth and tongue are fun to draw!

Tiny triangles are teeth. How would you draw the tongue?

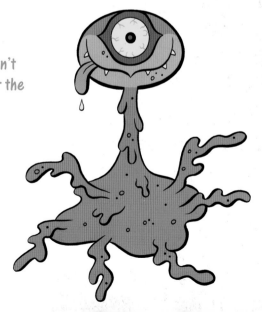

These appendages are sticky and jellylike, so use soft lines to draw them in any shape you want.

5. Use an ink pen or marker to trace only the lines you want to keep. Don't make the eye veins black—color them red or orange instead.

Erase the lines you don't need, or just color over the lighter ones.

6. Now color the rest of this monster!

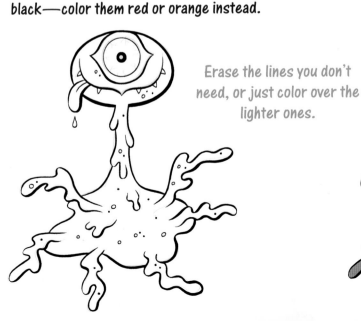

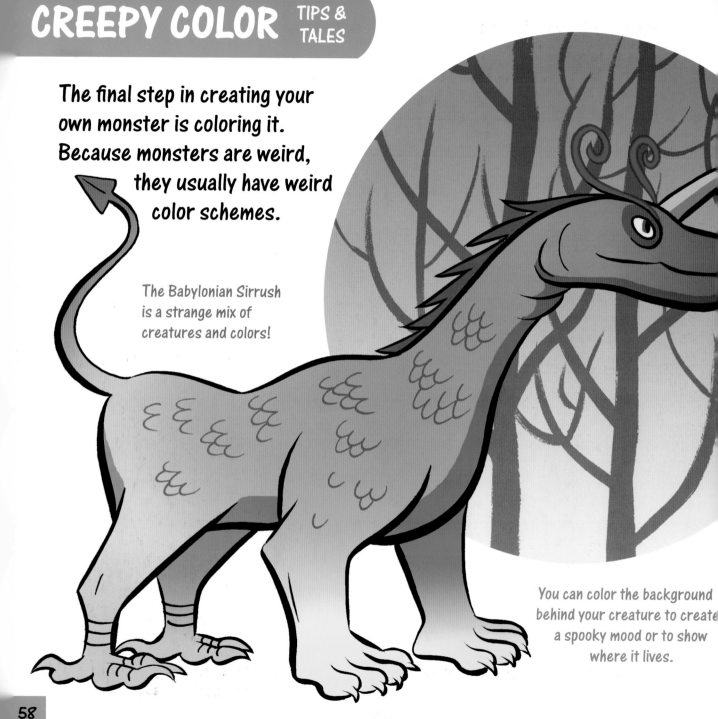

The final step in creating your own monster is coloring it. Because monsters are weird, they usually have weird color schemes.

The Babylonian Sirrush is a strange mix of creatures and colors!

You can color the background behind your creature to create a spooky mood or to show where it lives.

Because healthy human skin is a warm hue, cooler colors like blue, green, and purple look very strange and scary. Most famous monsters use these pale dead tones to look fearsome.

You can never go wrong with a creepy green!

Pale colors look ghastly.

Of course, a devilish red can be quite horrid.

Mixing a lot of clashing colors together has a freaky effect.

Color Techniques

Handy Dan is going to help us take a look at some colorful ideas.

All of the illustrations in this book were colored on the computer. To color yours this way, you need to scan your finished black and white drawing. Then you can use an illustration program to drop in colors. (Different programs have different ways of coloring.)

Computers allow you to mix any color you want, change colors around, and create fades and special effects. No mess to clean up, either!

Colored markers can create an effect similar to coloring on a computer. Just look at Dan now!

Markers are easy to use, and provide really bold, bright colors. Markers aren't the best for blending colors, though.

Colored pencils give you more control over blending colors and are great at creating texture.

You can get terrific shading effects from colored pencils, but they're not as good for smooth, bright colors. Always start with the lighter colors first if you plan to layer or blend colors.

Water-based paints let you blend colors and create lots of different shades. Paint bold, smooth colors, or dilute the paints with water for paler tones.

Paint can be very messy, though, and it can wrinkle your paper. Just like with colored pencils, start with the lighter colors first if you plan to layer or blend.

MONSTERS!

NAME:

TERRITORY:

DIET:

POWERS:

LIKES:

DISLIKES:

STORY:

By now you ought to be full of weird and wonderful ideas for creating your own monsters. I don't want you to lose a single spectacularly strange one! So scan, photocopy, or make your own version of the character sheet at left. Use it to record details about each of your fantastic creations.

There's a spot for describing the territory your monster prowls. (A castle? Laboratory? Cave?) Describe what it eats (feathers? homework?) and what weird powers it might have. (It can fit 42 doughnuts in its mouth?) You can also list its likes (a full moon?) and dislikes (lemonade?). Then write your monster's story.

Final Word

All the instructions in this book are only ideas to get you started. They're not rules for you to follow. Each of us has a unique and special imagination. What mischievous monsters are lurking in the shadowy corners of your brain? Set them free!

Thank Yous

Thanks to my wife, Elisabeth, and my two little monsters, Nora and Desmond, for all their support and inspiration.

Index